One of the King's Men

ESTELLE EVERINGHAM

Hardcover: 978-1-961438-40-8
Paperback: 978-1-961438-38-5
eBook: 978-1-961438-39-2
Library of Congress Control Number: 2023911968

This book is a work of nonfiction.

Ordering Information:

Prime Seven Media
518 Landmann St.
Tomah City, WI 54660

Printed in the United States of America

Losing someone you love is never easy. It's even more challenging to let go when the person you lose is your child. One of the King's Men is an aptly titled autobiography that thoroughly describes a man who transcended his life with compassion, love, and genuine good nature.

— Pikasho Deka for Reader's Favorite

One of the King's Men is Estelle Everingham's tribute to her son. Told in a loving mother's voice, the story begins with Cameron's miraculous birth; everything that follows in his journey is full of authenticity from his mother's point of view, including joy, humor, horror, and sorrow.

— Emily-Jane Hills for Reader's Favorite

This book is dedicated to my amazing son, Cameron, whose short life made these pages possible, and to his wonderful siblings, Katrina and Todd and their families.

It is presented for the enjoyment and inspiration of those who were born to create chaos in the devil's kingdom and for all whose lives make them dangerous to darkness.

Chapter 1

NEVER IN MY ENTIRE LIFE had I been aware that the doctor's words being spoken to me could be said to anyone, but here they were, being said to me. "Your baby has had no discernible pulse or heartbeat for 13 hours, and we cannot perform a caesarian section because your lungs will collapse and you'll die on the table. Your baby is dead. He's very large and is firmly stuck, so we are going to have to cut him up and take him out piece by piece."

Even in my drug-induced state, after 25 hours of labour, that statement sent shock waves through my mind and body. My brain raced to locate a possible alternative.

Right then, I realised that it was now early on Saturday morning, and the men at our church would be engaged in their monthly prayer breakfast. As I turned my head to ask my husband to go and phone the church, I noticed how pale he was. All colour had drained from his face, for he, too, had heard the doctor's words and was horrified to learn what was about to transpire. However, he seemed pleased to have a reason to leave the birthing suite and hurried to contact the church and ask for prayer. During the few minutes of my husband's absence, I kept a close eye on what the doctor was doing because I didn't want him to commence the procedure before my husband's return.

I saw the nurses placing grotesque-looking instruments in a row on the bench. Then, as an assistant clamped the velcro at the back of the doctor's gown, my mind whirled, and I felt like I was floating out of my body and drifting around the room.

The next moment my husband returned just as I emitted an earth-shattering, high-pitched scream. I didn't know it at the time, but the doctor had just cut me mightily in preparation for the dissection and removal of my baby.

I have no idea how a mother lives through such a barbaric procedure. Fortunately, I did not have to find out because, as the doctor turned aside to pick up his instruments, my baby slid out of his own accord and was caught by a shocked nurse just as he was about to land on the floor. He had the umbilical cord around his neck three times and required a little kick start of oxygen to get him breathing, but he was then displayed to me by a nurse who said in an amazed voice, "You have a 10 lb 2½ son, who seems to be perfectly alright." My son had been born straight into the prayers of the men at the church prayer breakfast, I knew right away that he would be special.

* * *

Cameron Nathan Richard Everingham was welcomed into the family by his sister, Katrina, aged 7½ and his brother Todd aged 4. He was a lovely baby, big and blond, with dark brown eyes and a gentle, sweet spirit. Provided he was clean, warm and fed, he was happy.

Cameron would cry and wake me up once or sometimes twice each night for a nappy change and a bottle. He always smiled at me, and we both enjoyed our "nightly dates" together until he started sleeping through the night at about eighteen months of age. I would refer to him as "my happy nappy chappy."

Regardless of the drama surrounding his birth, Cameron hit all his milestones either on time or early, was alert and curious, playful and entertaining and enjoyed babbling in his baby language. Trina and Toddy coo-ed and goo-ed with him, sang and played with him and loved him as he grew.

I loved each of my children very much and spent time with them, cared for them, prayed for them, dedicated them to the Lord, took them to church, and taught them about Jesus.

Even before Cameron was born, Trina and Todd loved to play church. Trina would sing and preach to their teddy bears. Todd would take up the offering, often shaking the bears upside down and telling them off if their offering seemed insufficient to him.

We were never an affluent family, as my husband, Philip, was frequently unable to work because of spinal problems and pain resulting from a congenital fault in his back. Our children had the necessities of life, but extras and treats were not available. Thus, we lived in the constant shadow of their father's extreme pain, hospitalizations, and operations, resultant drug dependency, anguish and turmoil. Through it all, the children were my rays of sunshine. When life was particularly tough, I would teach them about Heaven, because we lived in Hell.

One day, I heard a mother speak about listening for and recording her child's first sentence and then watching to see if it had relevance in the chifld's life. This was something I was determined to do. Unfortunately, I didn't hear Trina's first sentence because I was teaching school during her babyhood and missed the event. Todd, however, uttered a memorable and very apt first sentence; I recall walking past him as he lay in his bouncinette at age ten months. I was slightly surprised when my baby ordered me to "put the fan on one," Obviously, the weather was a trifle too warm for his liking at the time. Now, almost 40 years later, Todd is a successful businessman and entrepreneur who enjoys experiencing all the luxuries of life that he missed out on as a child. His comfort and the ability to inspire others to provide it for him feature high on his list of requirements. Good for him. I am so pleased for Toddy.

Therefore, I was not about to miss Cameron's first sentence.

The day arrived when Cameron was eleven months of age. We had a gathering of people at our home, probably for Todd's 5th birthday; Cameron was sitting in his high chair. Suddenly he picked up his spoon and struck it on the wooden tray of his chair until he had everyone's attention, then he eyeballed us all and announced, "God's not dead." This was not merely a first sentence but also a declaration that showcased perfectly how he would live his life. Now I knew for sure that this child was exceptional.

As Cameron became a one and then a two-year-old, his love of flora and fauna developed. He was particularly enamoured of the "big Chookies," as he labelled the pelicans he saw during our seven-week stay at Golden Beach, Caloundra when he was 17-18 months of age. When he would return after weekend visits to see his grandparents, Mee Maa and Do Do, Cameron would toddle around our backyard and pat each flower and bush, saying, "It's alright, I'm back now. Don't worry. I'm back again to take care of you."

I recall that when Cameron was about 18 months of age, I owned an old Valiant station wagon in which Cameron would sit in his baby seat and sing as we travelled.

His favourite song said, "Through our God, we shall do valiantly," which was most suitable.

However, as time passed, my Valiant was sold and replaced by a green Datsun coupe.

Cameron was just two years of age the first time I heard him singing in the back seat, "Through our God, we shall do Datsulently."

As a 2-year-old, he would always love to talk to me about going to Heaven; he would say, "going HOME to Heaven," rather than simply, "going to Heaven."

One Saturday morning, Cameron and I were in Coles Shopping Centre, buying groceries and talking about Jesus coming again. We had been speaking in this manner for about 15 minutes when Cameron informed me, in the harshest voice he possessed, "Mum, we've got to stop talking like this."

When I asked, "Why?" my 2-year-old told me that Jesus might just have been standing up, ready to come, but when He heard us talking, He would have had to sit down again. He said, "Jesus has probably been standing up and sitting down over and over again and it's all our fault. Jesus would be looking down and saying, 'Oh, bother, I can't come yet. I'll have to sit down again. Those Everinghams are expecting me!"

Cameron's reasoning for this idea was the Bible verse that states, "At such an hour as ye think not, the Son of Man cometh," Reasonably sound doctrine for a 2-year-old.

Cameron had just turned 3 when my suspicions about his uniqueness were confirmed.

One morning, my little blond toddler came out of his bedroom and stood in his pyjamas next to me with a strangely inquiring expression on his face. Then, holding out both his hands, with palms up, and pointing to each palm, he asked me, "Mum, why do they do the pictures of Jesus with the nail prints there and there when they're really here and here?" pointing to the inside of each wrist.

Having no real answer to this, I threw the question back to him and asked,

"Are they, Cameron? How do you know?"

A big, happy smile spread across his face as he replied, "When Jesus was in my room last night, and He held out His hands and He smiled at me, I saw them. They're here and here." pointing again at his wrists.

After considerable initial amazement, all I could think was, "What do I do with this child?"

* * *

Chapter 2

W HEN THE CHILDREN WERE 12, 8½ and 4½, I gained employment as a teacher at Westside Christian College, which all 3 of them then attended.

I enjoyed teaching very much, loved the staff and students and was delighted with the culture and beliefs of the school. Trina proved herself to be an excellent and competent student, attaining awards for her academic achievements and becoming a Senior Prefect. Tony showed excellent proficiency in all things mechanical and electrical. Also, he was voted House Sports Captain, much to our surprise. Cameron struggled academically but received awards for his efforts, which were always of a heroic standard. My hope for him was that he would find his niche, something at which he could excel. He had an invisible friend called Sonya, with whom he shared many happy moments and had stimulating conversations. Often he would mention to me things that Sonya had told him and I would think to myself, "Sonya is so wise. I wish I could meet her. She has such wonderful thoughts and ideas to share with Cameron."

During one school term, the athletic emphasis was on Cross Country running and the 10 to 12-year-old students all practised on the designated track before school, during P.E. lessons and in their lunch breaks for the day of the big event. When the day arrived, about 160 children aged 5, 6, and 7 gathered for the run. Among them stood one 5-year-old student, determined to run with them, –– Cameron.

Although he had never practised, was unfamiliar with the track and was wearing his leather school shoes, not joggers or running shoes, he had decided to compete. Much to everybody's surprise, he tore up the track like a pro and defeated all the 10-year-olds and all the 11-year-olds, plus about forty-five 12-year-olds. Although he was beaten narrowly by eleven 12-year-old boys, at age 5, he had found his niche.

During his primary school years, he became a champion runner in 100m, 200m, 400m, 800m, 1500m, 3klms, 5klms, 8klms, and cross country distances. As well he was a cycling champ and was also involved in swimming and Karate. We enjoyed cheering him on as he ran like the wind, with an amazingly focused look of determination on his face. One day, when Cameron was nine years old, he announced to me that Jesus had been in his bedroom the previous night and had been sitting on the edge of his bed.

Whilst attempting not to look too startled and like that was an everyday occurrence, I asked Cameron what Jesus had said to him. Cameron said that Jesus had said nothing at first, but then he said, "Mum, He put His hand in my stomach and pulled out a branch." Then Jesus said that the branch wasn't any good and he would throw it away." Immediately I thought of the Bible passage that speaks of not allowing roots, such as bitterness, to grow within us and the need to remove and discard them. I thought to myself, Jesus must have come to weed Cameron's garden for him. I mentioned this to Cameron and his reply was, "Yeah. That's right, I reckon." Then he ran outside to play.

Around this time, my husband Philip, Todd, Cameron and I moved to live on a 6-acre property near the small country town of Nanango. Trina did not accompany us because she was recently married and employed at a bank in Brisbane.

The boys had old dirt bikes they would ride around our extensive yard and did a little horse riding because a horse and saddle had come with the property.

Cameron also enjoyed riding his push bike and rode it into town on a memorable Sunday afternoon. He had been gone for a couple of hours, and I was beginning to wonder when he would return when he arrived, in a neighbour's ute, with his bike in the back.

He appeared flustered and proceeded to inform me about his afternoon's entertainment. He had been riding blissfully along a street in town when he was startled by a creature swooping at his head. Although he attempted to avoid his attacker, it persisted with its onslaught until Cameron dropped his bike and turned to see what was coming after him. When he found that his attacker was a magpie, Cameron knew he would have to find something to protect his head. He told me he ran past a few houses and found the perfect place, The Old People's Home. He thought, "I can go and knock on their front door and ask for help. Nobody in there will be fast enough to catch me if I encounter someone who tries to grab or otherwise scare me. I could outrun them all."

With that thought in mind, he knocked on the door and explained his predicament to an elderly resident, who told him to wait a minute and she would be back to solve the problem.

True to her word, she returned carrying a sturdy cardboard box in which she had cut two eye holes. Much to Cameron's horror, she placed the box firmly on his head, thanked him for his little visit and advised him to run back and collect his bike, then ride home wearing his new protective helmet.

"I thanked her very much for her help," he said, 'as I explained to her why I had chosen her door to knock upon.'

Then clad in the helmet, he had run back to his bike, but he had removed the sturdy box as soon as he was out of her sight. As he was riding home, trying to juggle the box, a neighbour's ute came up to him, and he was delighted to accept the offer of a ride home with his bike in the back.

One day, when Cameron arrived home on the school bus, he surprised me very much by announcing, "Sonya's so rude. Sonya brought Michael, and they talked off the top of my head. I might as well not have been there."

It was the first time I had heard Cameron say anything remotely negative about his invisible friend. I wondered just what Sonya had done to deserve such criticism, "When did this happen, Cameron?" I asked.

"Oh, when we were on the bus on the way home from school today," he replied.

"But I saw you on the school bus, Cameron. You didn't have any girl sitting next to you," I said. "Where was Sonya sitting?"

"On my shoulder," he replied, as though that was a perfectly normal way to travel on the school bus.

"Oh?" I said, "and where was Michael sitting?"

"On my other shoulder, Mum. They talked off the top of my head. I might as well not have been there," he repeated, indicating with his hand how they had spoken to each other right over the top of his head.

It was getting too much for me, so I asked him outright, "Cameron, who is Sonya?" But I wasn't at all prepared for his answer, "Sonya's my Guardian Angel, doesn't everyone have a Guardian Angel, they can see and talk to?"

"Well, no," I replied. That did, however, answer many of my questions about the brilliance of the concepts that Sonya had been discussing with Cameron for most of his life.

Life with Cameron was always interesting, but every so often he would say something that would stop me in my tracks. That was one such day.

When the boys were aged 15 and 11, Cameron and I moved back to the city, living on Brisbane's southside, whilst Todd boarded in Ipswich, where he had acquired an apprenticeship. When he turned 17 and obtained a car licence, he came to live with us and drove to and from Ipswich daily to continue his apprenticeship.

While at this location, Cameron began to train seriously for his running and commenced cycling. I enrolled him in Little Athletics at Springwood, where he ran sprints, distances and cross country. He and Todd attended Karate lessons as well.

Cameron would compete in a 100 km cycling race each Saturday and would frequently train on a nearly bush track during the week in preparation for his weekend ride.

One particular afternoon he returned from his training looking astonished and somewhat disheveled.

When I enquired as to why he looked like he'd been crawling through the bush, he told me that he'd been on his hands and knees on the track praising God and thanking Him for His protection and for saving his life.

As he said that, I wondered if someone had tried to attack him as he rode.

With a merry little twinkle in his eye, he informed me that he had been riding on a little-used section of the bush track, when, suddenly, a magpie had swooped at his head, much like the one in Nanango had done. Cameron's immediate response had been to duck his head right down near the handlebars and then dismount to try to chase the magpie away.

When he dismounted, he first noticed that a thin wire had been strung up across the track by someone at neck height. He thought a perilous obstacle had probably been put there to deter any trail bike riders who may have been riding there and annoying the surrounding residents with their noise.

Although he had not noticed the wire as he rode, he quickly realized that his action of ducking to escape the swooping magpie had prevented him from colliding with the wire and sustaining a severe injury or death. Hence his praise and thanks to God offered up from the bush track.

And his words to me, "God knew the exact, perfect thing to send to make me duck right down under that wire that I hadn't even seen.......

a magpie. If it had been Toddy, God would have had to send a beetle." We both thanked God for his protection and laughed together because the mighty Todd's fear of beetles and grasshoppers had been a standing joke at our place for quite some time.

Todd was and still is very accomplished, enterprising, organised, tough, and buff, but the appearance of a grasshopper or a Christmas beetle is enough to crash his world completely.

As a family, we attended church regularly, and Cameron, at 13, joined the church youth group and was, by his relationship with Jesus, quite an inspiration to the other young people, even though the age restriction on the youth group required that he be 15, not 13, to be eligible to join. His enjoyment of the church meetings was so pervasive that Cameron would frequently invite several of his teenage friends to attend. If they did not, he would purchase the DVD of the Sunday meetings and arrive at his friends' houses armed with the current DVD, and they would watch it together. Also, he would take notes of the sermon each week and use the notes to preach Sunday's sermon to his little group of friends at school during the lunch hour. From time to time, he would have school friends to visit at our home, where he would disappear with them up the ladder that led to his cubby house on the mezzanine floor of our triple carports.

Chapter 3

Fʀᴏᴍ Cᴀᴍᴇʀᴏɴ's ғɪʀsᴛ ᴅᴀʏ ᴀᴛ our local High School in year 8, he had taken a couple of pages of Revelation to school, torn out of an old Bible and kept in his shirt pocket. His reason for this was, "Mum, I'm going to a State High School, and I need to have some of God's word on me at all times for protection, but I'll remember that it's the Bible and not a tissue and I'll never blow my nose on it. Also, it needs to be pages from Revelation because that's the last book in the Bible, so it must be the closest book to Heaven, so I'll be alright if I carry some of that.'

During his year eight at High School, when he was thirteen, Cameron said something to me that was quite a surprise. I thought to myself at the time, "Well, you'd be the last of my children I would have expected to hear that from."

After wandering around, looking quite preoccupied for a couple of days, he had finally announced to me. "This getting prayed for stuff at church just doesn't work."

"Oh, how so?" I inquired.

"Well, I've prayed for three times for insomnia, and I still can't sleep," said he.

"Why can't you sleep?"

"I can't sleep for the light."

"What light?"

'The really bright light in my room.'

"Oh! Really? OK. How about I go to 'Spotlight' store and buy some dark material, and maybe Ann will make some curtains for your room?"

"Yeah, OK, Mum. That's a good idea, considering Ann sews with a sewing machine, and you sew with a stapler."

The mission was undertaken, and thick, navy blue cotton curtain material was purchased. My friend of then 12 years, Ann, or Annie Pannie, as Cameron called her, duly created some lovely, very suitable dark curtains which were hung over Cameron's windows.

The first morning after he had had a night with the new curtains, I ventured into his room to see if they had solved the problem for him.

I remember calling, "Cameron, Cameron, where are you?"

"I'm over here," replied a sleepy voice.

"Cameron, it's like a cave in here. It's so dark. Don't tell me you couldn't sleep for the light."

"I couldn't sleep for the light."

"What do you mean? It's dark.

How come you couldn't sleep for the light? What light?"

With some exasperation came, "Mum, when Jesus is in your room all night, He fills it with light, and He fills it with power, and you just can't sleep."

'What do you do while Jesus is in your room all night?" I asked.

"I just lie there in my bed, with my hands over my eyes for the light and try breathing in as much of His presence and power as possible."

During the course of that year, 1993, my husband and I had several conversations regarding Cameron, in which we both said that, as we watched him, we expected him to walk right off the ground, up into the air and continue walking in the air until he arrived Home in Heaven. It seemed he just didn't belong on this planet anymore because his focus and interest were increasingly on Heaven.

At the end of his year eight at school, he said, "Mum, I didn't do very well in my math exam."

"Oh, that's alright, you never do. Just as long as you did your best," I replied.

"But I wrote the teacher a note at the bottom of the exam paper," he said.

"Oh no," I thought, "whatever could he have written? Maybe I would never be able to attend a parent-teacher interview again without wearing a bag over my head.

"What did you write?"

"You don't need to get an A in maths to go to Heaven," said he.

That was very fortunate because he scored an E.

During the Christmas school holidays, Cameron announced that he would soon be going home to Heaven and that, when he got there, if people asked him what he had been doing on Earth when he left and went to Heaven, he did not want to have to say that he was attending a State High School. He would prefer to be able to say that he was going to a Christian school. He said that he knew that that would cost money and that he would get a job at the Golf Club up the road, cleaning or gardening, and pay for the school fees.

"No, you won't," I said, "If you want to go to a Christian school that much, then I will pay your school fees. I'll phone and ask for a prospectus from 3 or 4 local Christian schools, and you can see which one you would like to attend." I then reminded him that we had a 4-day holiday booked at the Sunshine Coast for two weeks into the new school year so that he could return to his current High School for two weeks, and we would organize his commencement at his chosen Christian school after the 4-day break. This pleased him very much, because it would allow him to bid farewell to his schoolmates in the new year.

Chapter 4

I HAD FOOLISHLY EXPECTED OUR 4-DAY break to be a time of peace and quiet relaxation. Oh, I should have known better.

Cameron managed to behave like an ordinary mortal until Sunday afternoon and then the atmosphere changed. At 1:15 pm on Sunday, February 6, 1994, he and I were in one of the resort spas together. I floated and relaxed while Cameron kept disappearing underwater to count how long he could survive without breathing. Suddenly he rose from the watery depths and fixed me with the kind of stare that heralded the outpouring of something magnificent.

Without pausing to consider my shocked amazement, "He announced, as water dripped from his blond hair down all over his face,

"Mum, I haven't got long to live."

After only two gulps of air, I inquired of him, "Do you think Jesus is coming back for us that soon?"

"No," he said, "It's not us. It's only me. I don't have long to live."

Having made that clear, he began to backtrack and perform a kind of life review, which majored on his forgiving people for hurtful things they had done to him throughout his life. Then my 14year-old commenced planning his funeral.

He said, "I want a no-frills funeral, not a yes-frills funeral, and I don't want flowers 'cause they'll make me sneeze.

All my favourite songs at church will have to be sung, especially "Celebrate. Jesus, Celebrate,"

"The Great South Land of the Holy Spirit" and the one that says. "Let the wind blow let the fire fall; we're in Revival."

Having listened carefully and agreed with all of that, I again thought foolishly that we could return to enjoying our time away. How wrong was I?" Cameron leapt out of the spa announcing, "Mum, we've got to go home now. We must leave and go back home to Brisbane right now."

This was too much.

"But we're booked in here until tomorrow. Then we'll go home, Cameron." I replied.

"No. We've got to go home right now."

I thought this required investigation because Cameron usually never argued with me. Just never.

"Why?" I asked. "What's so important that you reckon we've got to go home now?"

"Well," said he, "they have baptisms at the church tonight and I've never been baptized in water. I've got to be baptized tonight."

"Oh, Cameron," I replied, "Pastor Clark has baptisms organized about every six weeks. When we go to church during the week, you can speak to him and see if you can be baptized next time they're happening.

"No. I've got to be baptized today."

"Alright, Cameron," I said, "you know your father is lying down in our unit, suffering from a migraine, if you really want to be baptized today, go in and speak to him and see if he will come out and do it."

Away he went, only to return about five minutes later with his father in tow. Both were dressed in board shorts and both carried towels.

I was invited to join them at the resort pool as Phil baptized Cameron in the 3rd swimming pool of the Islander Resort at Noosaville on what turned out to be Cameron's last Sunday afternoon on Earth.

The following day we returned home from our mini holiday with a happy, newly baptized passenger rejoicing in the back seat.

*   *   *

As we travelled, Cameron discussed the movie, "Backdraft" which we had watched on TV the previous evening.

Cameron enjoyed the show, which portrayed the dangerous work carried out by firefighters as they attempted to save property and rescue people from being burnt.

He commented that if he were walking down the footpath and encountered a house on fire, he would rush inside and rescue anybody who was in there. He said that it wouldn't matter if he were burned to death because he would go straight to Heaven, but, whoever was inside might not know Jesus and Cameron's act of rescuing them would give them a chance to get to know Him before their turn came to die. Then they could go home to Heaven too.

When we returned from our mini holiday and the information arrived from the schools I had contacted, Cameron enrolled at

Southside Christian College, the school associated with the AOG church at Salisbury, pastored by Chris Peterson.

An appointment for an interview with the school principal was arranged for Tuesday, Feb. 8th, 1994.

I recall the appointment very vividly. Cameron was most excited about it and could scarcely wait for the time to arrive for us to set out. In the car on the way to the school, Cameron told me that if the principal asked him what career he wanted to pursue after leaving school, he would tell him that he wanted to be a preacher. I thought that seemed like a good idea, but I was not at all prepared for what else Cameron had in mind to tell him.

After about 20 minutes of talking about school, church, hobbies and interests, subjects etc., the principal told Cameron that he would be happy to have him in his school.

I imagined Cameron would thank him, shake his hand, and then prepare to leave.

Not at all. Cameron thanked him, said he was delighted to hear that, and asked, "Can I wear my earrings to school?" "Well," said the principal, "We only have girls here who wear earrings, not boys. Is your earring huge?"

"Oh no," said Cameron, "It's only a small one. But you won't let me wear it, right?" "Yes. That's our rule."

"OK," said Cameron, "I won't wear it at school. But you need to know that you will be very pleased to have me at your school. I don't know how well Southside performs at Inter School Sports Carnivals now, but your results are about to improve greatly. You'll be pleased that I decided to sacrifice my earring and come to your school because sports Days are about to make you proud."

The principal and his new sports star shook hands, smiled at each other warmly, and we left the office. It seemed to me that a truce had been negotiated along these lines. Yes, I will allow you to attend my school, but you must remove your small earring.

Yes, I will attend your school without the prized earring.

But whilst there, I will do my absolute best on Sports Days to increase your school's prestige, just so you realize that I'm doing you a favour, not the other way around.

As we made our way to the school uniform shop, I looked over at Cameron, thinking that he had sounded more like Todd than himself in his negotiating.

We purchased uniforms and Cameron would commence at Southside the next day without the earring.

The following morning, he was up bright and early, dressed and ready to be driven 5 kilometres to the school bus stop.

As I wished him well and waved goodbye, I couldn't help but notice how tall and athletic he looked in his bright uniform and how happy he was to be commencing at the Christian School finally.

During the day, as I was sorting through some of his belongings from the state school that he had just left, I discovered two pieces of Cameron's work from art classes and decided to ask him about them upon his return in the afternoon.

However, when I collected him from the bus stop, I could not get a word in. He was so full of the wonders of his new school. Yes, the school was outstanding, and the other boys had befriended him.

Yes, the teachers were all lovely and helpful; he could even hear and understand during the math lesson. The math teacher would help him to catch up, and the bus driver was a lovely fellow. His only difficulty with the school was that he couldn't locate the toilets. I advised him to make that his priority the next day.

After dinner that night, we discussed the two pictures he had drawn in his art class at his former State High School.

The first one was of an elegant and precise cross with one red droplet beside it, falling to the ground.

Cameron confirmed that he had indeed drawn it in art class at the State school and that it was the cross of Jesus. When I asked about the solitary red droplet, he replied, "Mum, one drop of Jesus' blood is enough to cleanse the entire world. It is so powerful."

Then he told me to look at his name on each of his belongings and all of his writing books from the school.

When I did, I was shocked to find that every time his name appeared, he had either drawn a cross beside it or written his name as Cameron J. C. Everingham or both. He told me that he always wrote his name like that because he is a child of his Father, God, so God should be acknowledged in his name, either with the cross or with J.C. for Jesus Christ, even though Cameron's middle names were Nathan Richard.

Then I asked about his second drawing, which looked intricate and involved. I told him it was an excellent drawing and asked him to explain it. He replied that that was exactly what his teacher at the state school had said last week and that he had told her all about it. "That's the Earth down there in that corner, and that is Heaven up there. When it's your turn to die, you zoom right up and because of the one drop of Jesus blood, demons are knocked out of the way and the devil is knocked off his feet and onto his side and you fly straight through to Heaven. Nothing and nobody can stop you because of the power of Jesus' blood.

I thought I ought to keep those pictures.

The next day was Thursday, and Cameron was up bright and early with his bag packed and ready for school.

As I drove him to the bus stop, I reminded him to seek out the toilets. He assured me that he would and told me not to bother to come to the bus stop to collect him in the afternoon because he could use the 5 km run home with his school bag on his back, as it would be good training for him.

Sure enough, he came jogging home after school, not even puffing slightly and was full of the continuing wonders of the new school.

Everything about it was marvellous, except he still hadn't found the elusive toilets.

After a short speech from Mother enumerating the benefits of finding the said toilets, he went to the kitchen to fill up his long, hollow legs, muttering something over his shoulder about the importance of his leg muscles, of which he was inordinately proud. He frequently spoke about these muscles, and I often noticed him performing his leg muscle exercises at the church while standing during singing.

I recall first noticing the famed leg muscles when Cameron ran in the Senior Primary cross-country race as a 5-year-old.

Chapter 5

THAT NIGHT, WHEN HE WENT to bed, there was no chance he was about to fall asleep. He'd been in bed for approximately half an hour when I heard him yelling, "Mum, Mum!"

Thinking to myself, "This child's not going to go to sleep," I ventured to his bedroom to be greeted by Cameron, lying in bed, but propped up on one elbow and gesturing towards one corner of his room and saying,

"Look at them, Mum. Look at them. They're talking to each other and they're smiling at me, and they're pointing Mum, and why are they red?" I looked everywhere but saw nothing; meanwhile, Cameron was keeping up a running commentary about them, saying they were angels, but wondering why they were red.

I even rushed outside to see if a car had just gone by, reflecting its red tail lights through Cameron's bedroom window, but there was no vehicle anywhere. Nothing was there at all.

When I returned to his room and told Cameron that there was no car outside with red brake lights, he said, "Of course not. Tail lights are red, but they don't talk, smile, or point at me, Mum. We must ask Pastor Clark why the angels are red."

Having said so, he bid me goodnight, rolled over and was soon asleep.

Off he went to school the following Friday, brimming with enthusiasm and armed with instructions to hunt for the toilets.

When he arrived home after another five km jog, he was almost beside himself with joy. No, he hadn't found the toilets; no they had not played sport at school in the afternoon. The reason for his great excitement was that they had 'chapel' at school that morning and even had 'worship,' I was informed. Furthermore, this would happen every Friday, and Cameron could scarcely contain his great happiness at this exciting prospect.

That evening, 11th Feb 1994, we went to the worship night meeting as usual. Philip played his trumpet in the band, as he always did, and Cameron and I enjoyed the session. This particular evening proved to be an extraordinary occasion for me. As we were in worship, much to my amazement, for the first time in my life, I experienced an amazing angelic encounter. I was lying on the carpet at church, under the power of God, when, suddenly, I could hear four trumpets playing when there should only have been one, played by Phil. I moved slightly to be able to look at the musicians, and even though my eyes were closed, I saw three tall angels, each over eight feet in height, standing behind Phil, and they were playing their trumpets too. Their trumpets were quite different from his. Two angels had ram's horn-type instruments, and the other had a long, golden heralding trumpet. I was most drawn to him. At that point, one of the angels approached me, and I asked him his name. He said, "I am Gabriel." I asked him the name of the heralding trumpet angel, and he said, "Never mind. He's just my mate." I looked at the "My Mate" angel and noticed that he had blond hair parted down the middle and flowing to the nape of his neck. I was somewhat surprised that he had a golden, narrow headband holding his hair in place. He wore a long, white garment with a golden sash at his waist and his tunic had long sleeves with four golden braids at the end of each sleeve, near his wrists.

After a time, which I would say may have been ten minutes, the angels began to fade before my vision I desperately wanted them to stay and recalled the Biblical incident of Jacob's angelic encounter. Now was the time to wrestle! That was easier said than done from a prone position, when one feels, at best, semi-conscious. I could see myself grabbing Gabriel's tunic and asking him, "Are you here because of our trumpet player, my husband, Phil?"

"No," he replied, "Don't worry about him,"

I begged him to please not go without showing me something of Heaven.

He said, "Alright. Have a look at this. Then we have to go."

Immediately, I found myself standing in front of my mother, Dorothy, my brothers Lloyd and Gary and my nephew, Terry, who was leading a dog. Each of these people and the dog had been dead for some years, my mother having died in 1967, twenty-seven years earlier. I found it most impressive that they all, except the dog, had their hands raised, worshipping God, and were filled with joy. I recall being quite spellbound by the raised hands, especially by seeing my mother doing this, as she had been the Brethren minister's wife and such outrageous behaviour would have been well and genuinely outlawed in my father's church. I glanced at the background behind them, which was a pale yellowy golden hue and then, much to my surprise, I said to Terry, "Whose dog is that?"

I would now suggest that if a Heavenly visit is on the agenda, having a decent list of questions would be a distinct advantage. I didn't even say "Hello."- Not to my mother or anybody. I just asked about the dog. Also, it wasn't speaking as we know it but rather transferring information from mind to mind.

Oddly enough, Terry didn't seem to find my inquiry unusual and informed me that this was my husband's dog from his childhood and that Terry just minded it for him.

With that having been established, the scene quickly faded, and I found myself on the church floor, trying vainly to describe to those around me what I had just experienced.

I told Philip and Cameron about what I had seen on the way home from the meeting. Phil wanted a complete description of the dog and took great delight in telling me that that dog had been called "Bouncer" and that he, as an 8-year-old boy or thereabouts, had been his proud owner.

Cameron, however, had a list of questions, "Mum, did you see the angels in Heaven? Did you see the streets of gold, the mansions, the River of Life?"

He almost leaped out of his skin and so excited to hear about Heaven that his mother granted this little preview. That night, I thought long and hard about this beautiful experience and inquired of the Lord why He had been so gracious to me, totally undeserving as I felt I was, and why it had happened right then.

The church we were in was experiencing a period of revival and signs and wonders were a frequent occurrence, but until that time, I had not been touched in this fashion.

The Lord reminded me that, on New Year's Eve, coming into 1994, we had attended a "Welcoming in the New Year" prayer meeting, which had continued until after midnight. After that meeting, which had happened six weeks before this particular night, Ps Clark Taylor's associate pastor, Ps Rob Pullar, had invited people to come forward to the altar and bring their requests for the New Year to God and have them sealed into their spirits by the laying on of hands. I had seen Cameron in the lineup, doing his leg muscle exercises, as he awaited his turn for prayer, and I knew immediately what I was going to ask of God.

"God, in 1994, please let me be able to walk and talk in the spirit realm, just like Cameron can."

On Friday, 11th Feb. 1994, God began to answer my prayer. Yahoo!!!

In memory of my extraordinary,
blessed and much loved son,

Cameron.

1/11/15.

Todd, 14 and Cameron, 10, on their dad's motorbike

Cameron, aged 5 wearing his dad's T-shirt.

Cameron, aged 10, with a bubble beard.

Cameron, aged 2 getting a helping hand from Toddy.

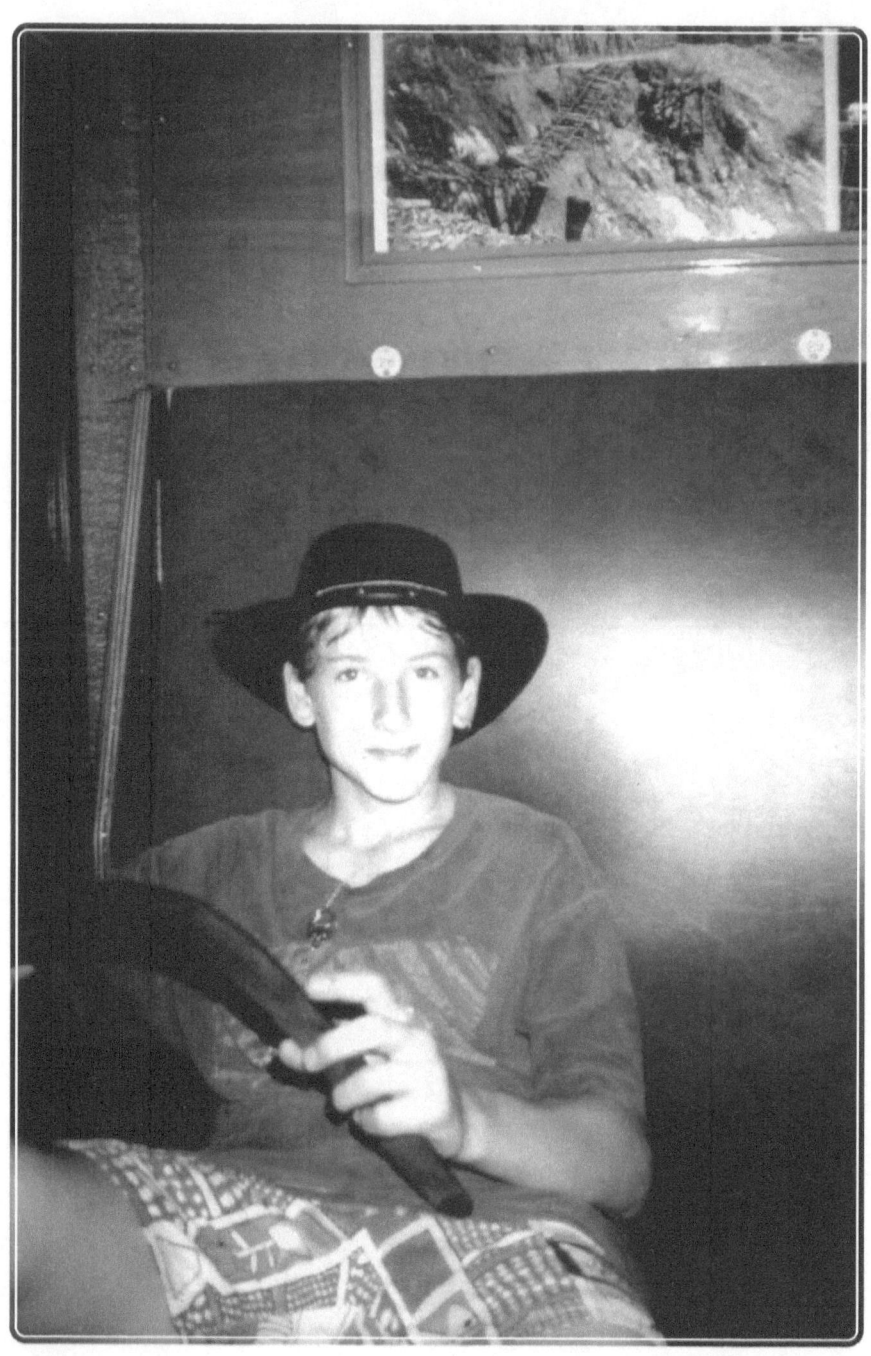

Cameron, aged 13 holding a boomerang.

Cameron, aged 6 in his Westside Christian College uniform.

Cameron, aged 9, and Katrina, aged 16, eating banana splits at the Big Pineapple on the Sunshine Coast.

Cameron, aged 14, with his mountain bike.

Cameron, aged 14, with his mum at the Great Barrier Reef.

Todd, 9, and Katrina, 12, sharing a dodgem car.

Cameron, aged four, wrestling with his grandfather, Do Do.

Chapter 6

ON SATURDAY, 12TH FEBRUARY, IT was my father's birthday, Phil and I were going to visit him at his farm property near Grafton in N.S.W. I asked Cameron if he wanted to accompany us, but he said, "No. I have a few friends to visit with the video from last Sunday's church meeting. Also, I've got two boys from the State High School coming, one at a time, to visit me in my cubby, and I can't be absent for that."

"Why's that, Cameron," I asked.'

"Just what is it that you do in your cubby?"

"Oh, Mum," he replied, as though I had just asked what he wanted on his sandwich, "Do you know that some of the kids at the State High School I went to play with Ouija boards and demonic stuff like that and they became possessed by demons? Well, they come to my cubby and I pray to cast the demons out. If I didn't do it, who would? So I have to be here. Also, I might get a chance to do a bit of jogging, and I need to do a hundred km bike ride this weekend. Say "Happy Birthday" to your Dad for me, please." Given that Cameron was 14 yrs 8½ months of age, and Todd, aged 18, lived about one hundred metres away, we left him at home.

On the way to Grafton, we listened to a tape by Don Franciscus and, for some unknown reason, played and replayed the track over and over again, where Don sang about, "When I wake up in the morning, I know there ain't nothing going to happen today that the Lord and I together can't handle."

We listened to that same track all the way home and found that Cameron had enjoyed his day and achieved everything except his one-hundred-kilometer ride.

Sunday morning dawned, and although it was fine, the slightly overcast sky indicated the possibility of rain later in the day.

Though the question was meant to be redundant, I asked Cameron whether he was coming to morning church. He said he would stay home and do his bike ride but then checked his mountain bike and found that it needed a part replaced before it could be ridden. So he dressed for church, and I complimented him for wearing his black and yellow striped T-shirt and black jeans instead of his red shirt with the hood that he seemed to like to wear to church all the time. His father promised to stop at the local bike shop on our way home from church and buy the required new bike part. He would fit it, he said, and Cameron could do his ride in the afternoon.

During church, Phil played the trumpet, and I enjoyed the meeting while observing Cameron doing leg muscle exercises to prepare for his ride. Several of the church musicians also observed him, who told me later that his face had been shining all through the church service. Following the end of the service, Phil packed away his trumpet, but we couldn't leave to go home because Cameron was in deep conversation with Ps. Clark Taylor.

Cameron came with us when he had finished talking to Clark, or "Sparky," as we frequently referred to him, and we journeyed to the bike shop on our way home. Unfortunately, the bike shop did not have the required part in stock, so Cameron said he would go for a jog instead.

During the meeting, a special presentation was delivered by Stan Smith, one of our church members, who told of the feeding programs he and his wife, Moira, had set in place in Asia. There they fed and cared for needy children and told them and their parents about the love of Jesus and how he had died for them on the cross, and how he wanted to forgive their sins and live in their hearts.

Cameron mentioned being very impressed by Stan Smith's feeding program but was most pleased that the people involved were being told about the love of Jesus. He said that if he had any money saved up, he would give it to Mr Smith for his program.

After having this discussion, Cameron announced that he was going for a jog and would be back soon. I told him I was about to prepare a quick lunch and that it would be ready in about 15 minutes.

When lunch was ready, Phil and I sat at the table, and Cameron's lunch was on a plate at the end of the table.

As expected, there had been a little rain, and the grass and streets were wet, but the rain had abated, and a pale sun was shining.

While we were eating and awaiting Cameron's return from jogging, we noticed the car of Todd's friend, David, being driven away past our home. Phil told me that Todd and David were going to Trina's house to tow Todd's car home because it had broken down and had been parked at Trina's place for a few days. They probably intended to try to repair it so that Todd could drive it to work the next day.

Then he asked me if I could hear the sound of a fire engine approaching.

I said, "No, and there wouldn't be a bushfire because the trees and ground are all wet."

Phil assured me that he could hear a fire engine coming from the left and a police car coming from the right.

I heard nothing.

Then he stopped, with his fork halfway to his mouth and said, "That'll be the boys (meaning Todd and David.) I'm going down to the end of the road to see. They can't have gone far, only to the corner." He said that maybe they'd had an accident and if so, he would phone me and let me know.

I stood by the phone in the kitchen with every nerve in my body jingling and wondered whether it was Todd or David who had been driving the car.

To my absolute horror, the phone rang, and I stumbled to answer it in what felt like slow motion.

Phil said, "David's car is smashed all over the road. There are police cars, tow trucks, a fire engine, and ambulances here, and the ambulance men are working on Todd by the side of the road. David is trapped in the front passenger seat, and the tow truck men are using the jaws of life to get him out. I'm going to look in the car and see how David is. I'll be home in three minutes, and we'll have to go to the hospital with the ambulance men and Todd. Please write a note for Cameron and let him know where we're going and leave it on the table. That way he'll see it when he comes back home from jogging. Tell him that Todd looks like he'll be alright, but the ambulance men fit a collar around his neck and it appears he has broken his arm.

Still, in slow-motion mode, I got my bag and keys together but did not feel like writing a note for Cameron, so I didn't.

A couple of minutes later, Phil arrived home. His face looked pinched and grey. My immediate thought was, "Oh, no. Toddy's lost a leg or something."

But he just stood there in the doorway saying over and over.

"Cameron's dead, Cameron's dead. Cameron's dead."

I replied in Cameron's defence, "Cameron can't be dead. Cameron's jogging."

As he hurried me out the front door, Phil told me that he was walking to the smashed car to see how David was when he heard a young lad in the great crowd of on-lookers mentioning the blond boy lying dead on the back seat of the car. Phil said he couldn't think who that could be because the only blond boy he knew was Cameron and Cameron was jogging. He then told me, as we drove to the accident scene, how he had approached the car and had seen Cameron lying across the back seat, perfectly still and dead, with his seat belt still on. He told me that he had opened the back door of the car and said, "It was good that I kept holding onto the car door because the wave of peace that came out of that car and hit me in the face was so powerful that it almost knocked me right over."

He said in quite an uncomprehending voice that he had heard Cameron speaking to him from above in the air, saying, "I'm alright, Dad, no one can hurt me now."

I decided right then that when I arrived at the accident scene, I would command Cameron's spirit to get back inside his body and for him to come to life again. I would do it in Jesus' name and didn't care who saw or heard me or what an idiot I might look like. That was what I was doing.

As I attempted to prepare myself for this, with perhaps one minute of driving time remaining, I thought I should ask Philip how badly Cameron was injured so I wouldn't be too shocked when I saw him.

"He must have died immediately," said Phil, "because around his eyes was just beginning to bruise and there was only one drop of blood visible on him. It's on his ear lobe from where his earring was ripped out in the accident!"

Upon our arrival, Philip went to ask the ambulance men if we could travel to the hospital with them, but they said we would need to follow in our car. I was wandering about like a lost sheep, with my spirit on high alert, trying to locate Cameron's spirit to order it back into his body, but it was just not there. It had gone, gone, gone.

I was so distressed that I could barely hold myself upright, so I looked for something to lean on. A policeman was standing in the middle of the road, directing traffic around the crash, so I flung my arms around him. As I stood there, unable to find Cameron's spirit, I thought to myself that I must go close enough to the car to see a piece of Cameron's black and yellow striped shirt; otherwise, I would never believe he was dead and would spend my whole life waiting for him to come home from jogging. I took one, only one step towards the car and bang. I saw it all again, in the whole panorama. My mother, Lloyd, Gary, Terry and the dog in Heaven, as they'd been on Friday night. Then I heard the audible voice of God speaking to me from above my right shoulder in an authoritative and mild tone. "They were his welcoming committee."

My dismay, horror and shock at not being able to locate Cameron's spirit immediately dissipated as I said to God, "If Heaven has been standing at attention waiting for Cameron since Friday night, who am I to call him back?"

I took the remaining four or five steps to the car, looked at the shirt and noticed the blond hair and lack of injuries and felt at peace, even though I knew I would miss Cameron incredibly, especially his amazing walk with God and the astounding revelations he used to share with me, from Sonya. There would be many, many tears for Cameron, but now my concern was how was I going to be able to break the news of Cameron's death to Toddy, how badly injured was Toddy and how would he ever be able to survive this tragedy, considering he had been the driver. I knew that Todd would be devastated because he loved his younger brother so much and would stand up for him and protect him within one inch of his own life. I also knew that Cameron loved Todd amazingly and he had often told me how he always felt safe with Toddy, because Todd was so strong and would always look out for him. Todd had a very definite "big brother" mantle and always kept a watchful eye on Cameron and tried and hoped to mould Cameron in his image. Cameron loved to float along in Todd's considerable wake, saying little, adoring Todd and responding to him as would Jesus, which I'm sure ticked Toddy off not a little.

There isn't anything going to happen today that the Lord and I together can't handle!

Chapter 7

P HIL PHONED TRINA AND TOLD her what had happened. Her reaction was to scream and collapse, absolutely understandably. She, as the eldest, had always been a great help to me and had desired to be a second "Mummy" to her younger brothers. Cameron was delighted in that role. Then there was Todd. I'm pretty sure he found being subject to one mother to be more than sufficient and was not about to be mothered by his big sister, too, once he was about five years old.

One notable exception to that rule occurred one day when a neighbouring thug was foolish enough to give Todd a tough time and pick on him unmercifully.

Regardless of Todd's attempts to persuade this boy of the folly of his annoying behaviour, it took Trina running down the street, clinging him over the head with a skateboard, for him to decide to leave Toddy in peace. I wish I had seen that, as it will never happen again.

We saw Todd on a trolley in the hospital, and he immediately asked me if Cameron was alright. When I told him that Cameron had gone home to Heaven, I was well aware that Todd was smashed to the core upon hearing this news, and I was pretty tempted to take a step or two backward as I fully expected him to rise off the trolley, fly around the room a few times and then throw himself out the nearest window. I assured him that Cameron had not suffered and that he would be thrilled to be in Heaven. He was safe and could not be hurt; we knew where he was and he had always wanted to be. I told Todd not to blame himself and that I loved him beyond his ability to comprehend, that he should rest and concentrate on getting better and that everything would be alright.

David's injuries had been extremely severe because part of the car's roof had embedded itself in his head. I was told that he had died three times during the first night, but he was revived.

Todd had injured his hip and badly broken two bones in his left arm, which required inserting a metal plate. Also, he had struggled so hard with the steering wheel trying to avoid the collision that he had stretched the nerve behind his left eye, causing it to turn right in, producing a very cross-eyed effect.

Cameron's autopsy showed that he had sustained many internal and severe injuries to his brain. He had a broken left arm and nine ribs, courtesy of his seat belt. He also had four breaks to the orbital bones around his eyes. He had died very speedily because his aorta had been wrenched out of his heart. I was shocked and amazed to learn that he had suffered a dislocated leg on impact but that the great strength of his mighty leg muscles had been sufficient to pull his leg entirely back into place. My word, wouldn't he be impressed with that as he looked down from Heaven? "Remember, mother, the leg muscles are important!"

We left the hospital, encouraged Todd to recover, and attended church that evening. However, we had a devastated, tearful, collapsed daughter, an injured son in the hospital and another son in the morgue. But where else could we possibly go? A pastor and his wife, the Holmes-Brownes, had met with us at the hospital; many in the congregation had seen the news report of the accident on television. People were shocked, horrified, and tearful, but very kind and compassionate, especially towards Phil as he strove to play that trumpet.

The next day, Clark Taylor visited our home to arrange to conduct Cameron's funeral. When I informed him about many of the highlights of Cameron's life and of his remarkable relationship with God, Clark's exact words to me were, "I, as an international evangelist, would have given my right arm to have a few drops of what God poured all over Cameron's life, in bucketsful." He then told us that Cameron's conversation with him after the meeting the day before had consisted of Cameron saying to him, "Clark, I want to be a preacher. Can you show me how to get started?" Clark had told Cameron that he would bring some information and bookwork to get Cameron started, when they both attend the coming Wednesday night meeting. But instead, on Wednesday, Clark buried Cameron.

Cameron's request to Clark was the last he had made on Earth.

When we discussed the upcoming funeral, Clark was perplexed, asking, "How can I do a funeral service for Cameron? Cameron was so alive. He was a fast runner and could ride a bicycle or a motorbike like the wind. He wanted to be a preacher. On Wednesday, can I preach for Cameron?"

I told Clark that he had better preach, or Cameron would come jumping down out of Heaven and grab him by the throat. So we had a celebration service in honour of Cameron's fourteen years of life and Clark preached.

In Cameron's absence, I told Clark about Cameron's recent angelic visitation and asked him, "Why were they red?" Clark said that he didn't know but that he would ask God. He returned with the answer that they were red because they had brought Cameron a blood covering from the Mercy Seat in Heaven. After all, Cameron was marked out for glory.

Perfect.

Chapter 8

S EVERAL HIGHLIGHTS STOOD OUT TO me as I reflected on the last few weeks of Cameron's life. Firstly, I was thankful that Cameron had had the opportunity to attend the Christian School as was his desire and had I not taken notice of this request when he first mentioned it, he would have missed out altogether. Secondly, I was so glad that Cameron had prevailed upon his father to baptize him on his last Sunday afternoon on Earth. He couldn't be baptized the next time Clark scheduled baptisms. He didn't have the time. Amazingly, Cameron had died on Sunday, Feb 13, at 1:15 pm, precisely a week to the minute after he had told me in the spa that he didn't have long to live. Two other matters I looked into that first week yielded quite surprising results. First, I scaled the ladder to check that none of Cameron's possessions remained in his cubby. No. There was nothing to be seen except a large sign written with a thick black felt pen in Cameron's handwriting stating, "THIS CUBBY IS PROTECTED BY THE BLOOD OF THE LORD JESUS CHRIST FOREVER AND EVER. AMEN."

Then I obtained a baby names book to search for the meaning of Sonya, Cameron's inspirational and wise guardian angel. I discovered that Sonya means Wisdom. WOW!!!

Wednesday, 16th Feb; the day of Cameron's funeral, finally arrived. We had a small, private burial ceremony at a local cemetery, attended by family and close friends. Then we would have the Celebration Service after that at church. I chose this arrangement because I thought there might be children at the service at church and I didn't want them to be intimidated by the presence of the coffin.

The church was filled with congregants, family, neighbours and friends. Also, there were teachers and students from Westside Christian College, where I had taught and my children had attended years earlier. The State High School was represented by students and some teachers, including the math teacher, to whom Cameron had written the note about not needing to get an A in maths to go to Heaven. Southside Christian College sent a large bus full of year nine students together with staff members and administrators. There were also patched-up Christian Motor Cycle Club members in attendance with their Harleys lined up outside. That group had been established about eight months earlier by Phil, Todd, Cameron, a local Christian police senior sergeant and two bikers from Parklands Church, which was pastored at the time by the esteemed Ps. Rodney Jobe.

Our daughter, Katrina, was Ps. Jim Williams P.A. at his Springwood church, where she led the worship, and her husband sang and played electric guitar. They joined with our church musicians, including Phil, on the trumpet, for the celebration service. Todd was discharged from the hospital in time for the occasion and a young lad played the drums, using Todd's drumsticks because Todd's arm was in a sling and he was very cross-eyed.

I presented the Eulogy, a 45-minute education for all, on the life and times of Cameron and Clark Taylor, preached on "Who Will Take the Baton of Faith From Cameron's Hand and Run With It?"

This was the only funeral service I've ever attended in my life where about 100 young people responded to Clark's invitation to come forward and dedicate their lives to Christ. Many of them were from Southside Christian College, Cameron's chosen school, which he attended for three days, not even long enough to locate the toilets. Others were friends to whom Cameron had re-preached Clark's sermons at the State High School and yet others were boys who Cameron had visited, armed with his church videos. He must have been making handstands in Heaven.

As Cameron had told me in the spa at Noosaville, just ten days earlier, when he was planning his funeral, that he didn't want flowers because they'd make him sneeze, people responded to an invitation to donate money in Cameron's honour to Stan Smith's Feeding Program in Asia instead of purchasing flowers or other tributes.

Two nights later came the Friday night worship service, one week from the night I met Gabriel and the My Mate angel and saw Cameron's welcoming committee in Heaven.

Chapter 9 ⚜

ON THIS FRIDAY NIGHT, GOD really amazed me. While we were in worship, he gave me a glimpse of Cameron in Heaven. He was wearing his green and yellow board shorts and his black and yellow striped T-shirt. Unfortunately, I hadn't learned a thing during the week, so instead of talking to Cameron and telling him how much I loved him and missed him, I thought, "That's not right. He went to Heaven wearing his black jeans. Those board shorts are folded up in the second drawer in his wardrobe. He can't be wearing them in Heaven."

Even though I didn't speak a word, my thoughts were read because God's voice replied, "Are they? You won't find them!"

I informed a shocked Philip about this vision on our way home from church and we quickly rushed inside to inspect the wardrobe drawers in Cameron's bedroom. Although I knew perfectly well that I had washed, dried, ironed, folded and placed these shorts, together with the red shirt with the hood and several other garments in Cameron's second drawer just the previous afternoon, they were indeed nowhere to be seen. Oh, the red shirt with the hood and the other clothes were there, but there were no green and yellow board shorts anywhere.

Although we emptied all five of Cameron's drawers, practically dismantled his wardrobe and also swept beneath it, no board shorts were there to be found.

Phil and I just looked at each other silently, wringing our hands. This was too odd, just too, too peculiar.

I thought to myself, "I don't think that this agrees with my doctrine," while Phil picked up the red shirt with the hood and speculated, "If he was going to come back and swipe anything, wouldn't you think it would be this shirt? He always liked to wear this." Then he added, "If he comes back here and pinches my trumpet, he'll be in the worst trouble!"

I must say that I had never given much consideration to this type of eventuality before. I had always assumed, I guess, that once a person had indeed died and gone to Heaven, they should reasonably be able to be relied upon to stay there at least. Obviously, not in all cases.

Todd's immediate response to hearing about this situation was to say, "Mum, don't tell too many people about that. They'll think you've finally lost your one remaining marble!"

To me, this was all extraordinary and highly unexpected, and I began to ponder it and speak about it to God.

I recalled that about six months previously, God had told me that He wanted to take me through a very deep valley. He had shocked me by asking me whether or not I was willing to go.

My reply had been that I would go provided. He came with me, and He held my hand and that, in the valley, I would meet Him as the Lily of the Valley.

I wondered whether this incident was connected to that. I knew, of course, that it all related predominantly to my New Year's Eve request that I be permitted to walk and talk in this spirit realm like Cameron could, but WHAT was this??

I soon discovered that I could sense Cameron's presence in the meeting during many Sunday worship services. That was wonderful but also concerning because I know that we, as Earth-bound Christians, are not to try to communicate with the dead. But I had not done that, and this was something that was just happening, not at my request at all. On one particular occasion, both my friend Ann and I were well aware of Cameron's presence in the church, and we both knew that he was sitting on the steps leading up to the platform.

Clark Taylor was in America, and Ps. Rob Pullar was preaching that morning. We both kept an eye on Rob as he frequently moved about and went quite close to where we knew Cameron was sitting. Suddenly, he stepped right where Cameron sat, and we watched in great surprise as he actually tripped over Cameron and then struggled to adjust his steps to save himself from falling.

We spoke to Rob after the meeting, and he said that he had been aware that there was a presence on the platform steps, but he'd had no idea it was Cameron.

As he recovered, Todd told his father and me that the accident had occurred because, as he was driving along the road, just around the corner from our street, the back passenger-side tyre had blown out. That tyre was right below where Cameron was sitting. Todd and David had passed Cameron as he jogged along the footpath and David had called out to Cameron and asked him to accompany them on their trip to tow Todd's car. David said they could use Cameron's help because he had strong muscles. Ever keen to assist, in he hopped.

With a blown tyre and the resulting difficulty in controlling the car, Todd attempted to steer it to the opposite side of the road, where there was lots of room to change the tyre. He said there was only one other car on the road, driving towards him and at quite a distance. Todd needed to cross in front of this car to get to the safe expanse of footpath and he kept trying to eyeball the approaching driver so that he could determine that this driver could see what Todd was trying to do. "But Mum, he never looked up. He never looked up. He was fiddling with something down near his dashboard and he never looked up. - Maybe it was the air conditioning switches or the car radio or something, Mum, but he just kept coming straight for us and he never looked up."

As the car Todd was trying to control was doing about 1 km an hour sideways, sliding across the wet road, and the other car was coming fast, Todd tried to turn his car around so that the other car would hit the back of them. He got it halfway around, and the other vehicle, which could just have driven around him, slammed into the passenger side, hind-quarter of Todd's car, right where Cameron was sitting. The police estimated the impact to have been about 200 km per hour. Even if Todd was doing 20 kms an hour, rather than only one, another car was moving.

Todd told me that, immediately before the impact, when there was nothing more that he could do to prevent the crash, he had let go of the steering wheel and turned to face Cameron.

Cameron had said to him, "I love you, my friend. Goodbye." - they looked at the car about to plough into him and laughed!

This was entirely too much for Todd, who announced, "Mum, no 14-year-old can die laughing!!!"

I asked him whether he thought Cameron had been looking at the car coming to kill him or the angels coming to take him home to Heaven and Toddy replied, "It would have to have been the angels, Mum."

A day or two after having had this conversation with Toddy, I said to God, "Please don't tell me that my son was killed in that car because another car smashed into him and turned all his internal organs into mush. Please tell me you sent your angel to take his spirit just before that car connected with him." God told me that, yes, the angel took him just before the impact, and Cameron wasn't there to be killed by that car because he had already gone. No wonder I hadn't been able to find his spirit at the accident scene.

I thought of the Bible account of the stoning of Stephen and understood it perfectly. However, I still said to God. "Thank you for that. Now, please show me how it happened."

Immediately, I was shown the actual accident. The car came quickly, and Cameron looked up at the angel and smiling, then laughing. I asked to see it once more, in slow motion. As I watched the angel's hand coming forward to grab Cameron's hand, I was struck by a very peculiar but familiar feeling.

"One more time, Lord," I pleaded. This time I knew what I was looking at. Sure enough, there he was, the angel with the four gold bands around his white tunic sleeve. – My mate angel!!!

God told me, "We sent My Mate to transport your mate to Heaven." God doesn't miss a thing, you know. From the day of Cameron's birth, his paternal grandfather, Barry, or Do Do, as Cameron had referred to him, always called Cameron "My Little Mate" and, as he grew bigger, simply, "My Mate." Cameron and his grandfather had been very close, the best of mates.

How good is God????

My next incredible Heavenly encounter occurred, not surprisingly, at another Sunday worship service.

As I stood there, a tall, blond-haired angel appeared at the distance, facing away from me. Because this angel had almost shoulder-length hair, I determined it was female.

However, as I approached 'her' from behind and 'she' turned to face me, I could see that I had been quite mistaken. This was no female angel. He had what we would refer to as a "5 o'clock shadow" covering his face. I had never considered that angels might need a shave from time to time, but this one did. Ha! I knew him. It was the My Mate angel once again.

He said to me gently. "You know me as the My Mate angel, but my real name is Sonya. I have been Cameron's guardian angel since before his birth. I sense you have been concerned, so I wish to speak to you about your son, Cameron."

I just knew this would never be an ordinary conversation, either.

"Well," he said, "You have been wondering about Cameron and the fact that he frequently leaves Heaven. I wish to commend you for your raising of him. Of course, he arrived here in Heaven after his Earthly demise because his spirit had been renewed, regenerated, and born again, but he came back to us with so much of his soul realm intact, and that is quite unusual. It was almost all intact, so much so that he entered on a level whereby we could give him the job of being in charge of a galaxy, so he can be trusted to come and go at will."

I felt that I might collapse simply because of the magnitude of Sonya's words, but he was not yet finished and went on to say. "Before we sent Cameron's spirit to Earth at the time of his conception, we had looked at his assigned number of days and were unsure whether to send him to you because his number was so small. But we decided that, though his days would be few, having him, even for such a short time, would be more of a benefit than a difficulty to you, and so, because he was such a pliable, gentle yet strong and obedient spirit, we gifted you with him. That is why he can come and go."

To say that I felt that a feather could have knocked me down is a serious understatement of fact. Here was Cameron's angel, Sonya, explaining eternal, Heavenly mysteries to me. To me. Such an unmerited honour!

Chapter 10

OVER THE ENSUING MONTHS AND years, Ann and I experienced many times when we knew that we could detect Cameron's spirit in our Earthly atmosphere.

On one occasion, even, we experienced an incident whereby we visited a shopping centre in Sunnybank Hills in Brisbane and parked the car in a particular, usual position. When we returned to the car park, however, the car was nowhere to be seen in the area where it had been left.

We both became aware simultaneously that Cameron was around and that he was having a bit of fun with us. It took us about 20 minutes to locate the car, which was far from where we had parked it and it was facing the complete opposite direction. All in all, it was an unnerving yet strangely delightful and memorable experience that day. – One about which we still chuckle.

My most remarkable and blessed experience with Cameron came, however, one Sunday morning at church; the congregation was singing "Lift Up Your Head to the Coming King," followed by "Praise is the Power of Heaven" and then "Majesty." As we sang, I became frozen in place and stuck to the spot. I didn't and couldn't move a muscle. I remember Ann asking me if I was all right, but I could offer absolutely nothing by reply.

Then, as I stood there stock–still, I felt the weight of an arm around my shoulder and reaching down to my waist. I heard Cameron say, "Take a step with me, Mum." So I attempted to take one step.

Immediately, I found myself standing on a long street of gold with Cameron next to me. From our left came a vast procession of old testament saints who were approaching where we stood and were singing "Lift Up Your Head to the Coming King." From the right came a host of New Testament saints, singing "Praise is the Power of Heaven." Before us was a large golden entrance that led into a vast, banked auditorium, where thousands of worshipers sang "Majesty" together with many dancing angels, the rows of saints began to enter through the golden doorway to swell the congregation inside.

"Come on, Mum," said Cameron, "Let's go in."

We stepped through the doorway and I stared in astonishment at the vast assembled crowd, wondering wherever we would find a place to sit. Eventually, I spied two seats together, high up in the auditorium, almost in the rafters. As I was puzzled about how we could make our way to these distant seats, we were there through the enormous crowd.

They were undoubtedly two vacant seats, but we didn't sit down. Neither did anyone else sit because God was in the house. So was Jesus. They were both seated on thrones, but everyone else stood in reverence and awe. Clouds of the Glory of God swirled around the thrones while beautiful, majestic music and pure light streams bathed the room.

Several angels entered and approached the thrones. They carried large silver trays from which fragrant, visible, wispy clouds ascended gently to God's nostrils. These were the prayers of the saints on Earth.

This worship service was so magnificent that it was well beyond the ability of my physical senses to contain its glory.

We seemed to be in this wonderful place for many hours, yet for only a few seconds, all simultaneously.

I felt as though I would love to remain there forever, but also, I was relieved when it was time to go because I feared that at any second, my body would blow apart, simply explode.

I have no idea how we made our way out of there, through the enormous crowd, but I finally found myself standing in church, clinging onto the back of the seat in front of me to keep myself from collapsing. Although I struggled to open my eyes, I couldn't see anything in the church building. All I could see were scenes from Heaven. My eyesight remained like that for several weeks. It was about three weeks before I would drive my car because I couldn't see the road or the traffic. It was as though my eyes were covered by a layer of something which filtered out the sights of Earth.

Also, I could not string a rational sentence together without enormous difficulty for almost a month. Yes, I could think, more or less, but I absolutely could not function. It was as though my body and senses had been ruined as far as life on Earth was concerned.

Desperate to re-acclimatize me to life on Earth, I tried to centre myself by meditating on the most mundane, Earthly thing I could envisage to bring myself back to "a rational state."

Thus, my first car journey was to K-Mart, where I strolled up and down the Barbie doll aisle, trying hard to focus on the dolls instead of seeing Heaven, angels, saints and God's throne. I stayed there for hours until I could focus on my surroundings sufficiently to drive myself back home.

From that time on, my Earthly life strengthened, little by little and Heaven began to recede slowly and gradually.

I found that whilst my spirit remained amazingly susceptible to the atmosphere of Heaven for three or more years, I could function in my Earthly life well enough to get by. However, I am well aware that even now, were I to hear those same three songs in the same order as they had been sung in Heaven, I could not guarantee that I would be able to remain upright but would likely become a dazed heap on the floor.

During the months following Cameron's departure, we searched his wardrobe repeatedly for board shorts, but found nothing.

When we relocated to another house in Brisbane, and the wardrobe was about to be removed entirely, I thought how foolish I would feel if there they were, somehow stuffed down behind it.

However, when the removalists shifted that wardrobe, there were no board shorts. Instead, there was a wooden cross that Cameron had made. I did inquire of God regarding the travelling board shorts and He replied, "You pray and expect things, such as finances or healing, to come from my Heaven and manifest themselves on your planet, why would you think it would be more challenging for us to arrange to have articles leave Earth and arrive in Heaven? Cameron left Earth and came to Heaven, didn't he?"

Early in 1994, a man from our church was busy writing a book called "Footprints" and was kind enough to ask if he could dedicate it to Cameron. When I agreed, he wrote;

Dedicated to Cameron Nathan Richard Everingham, one of the King's Men, Could I do less?

"Mum, when Jesus is in your room all night, He fills it with light, and He fills it with power, and you just can't sleep."

So said Cameron, my 13-year-old son, through whose short life God walked and talked and left His glorious fingerprints everywhere.

Cameron, my 3rd child, was a uniquely blessed boy who lived his life like he was starring in the 29th chapter of Acts.

Nowhere else in my life, either as a P.K. (preacher's kid) or as a school teacher with forty-one years of experience, did I ever encounter a young boy with so remarkable and vivid a relationship with the Heavenly realm.

Enjoy this complete factual account of his time on Earth as related by his mother, whose life was forever impacted by her contact with this very special one of the King's men.

This is Cameron's story, and welcome to it.

www.ingramcontent.com/pod-product-compliance
Lightning Source LLC
Chambersburg PA
CBHW020921140626
46545CB00015B/1104